A **Spirituality** of
Work

Catholic Bishops' Conference of England and Wales
Committee for the World of Work

CATHOLIC MEDIA TRUST

Contents

Foreword

The World of Work Committee of the Catholic Bishops' Conference of England and Wales offers this booklet as a contribution to the awakening of the Catholic Church to the blessing given the human race by God by the gift of work. The members of the Committee, who are themselves laity and workers, are well aware of the discontinuity in the perception of many workers between the experience of work (or unemployment) and the fulfilling of God's purpose for them. It is my hope that this modest volume will be of help to many. The mix of text and quotations from Scripture, the teaching of the Church and from experience, I hope will encourage reflection, lead to prayer and finally to conviction about the blessing of work.

I am deeply grateful to each member of the Committee for their contributions to this work. Inevitably, not all the riches of their experiences and observations could be included. This will serve to remind those who use this booklet in a spirit of discovery and reflection that work is part of the mystery of God's loving will for the human race. May this small publication help all who use it to explore yet further that mystery.

+ John

Bishop John Jukes OFM Conv
Chairman, Committee for the World of Work

1. Work in the sacred scriptures

'Whatever your task, put yourselves into it, as done for the Lord and not for your masters, since you know that from the Lord you will receive the inheritance as your reward.'

(*Colossians* 3:23-24)

A gospel of work

The Catholic Church draws its authoritative teaching from two key sources: the sacred scriptures (defined in the *Catechism of the Catholic Church* as the speech of God as it is put down in writing under the inspiration of the Holy Spirit), and sacred tradition (the living transmission of the apostolic faith under the guidance of the Holy Spirit). Among other things, the Church, from these two 'distinct modes of transmission', is able to expound what Pope John Paul II has termed the 'Gospel of Work'.

The Bible begins with God at work, and everywhere throughout the scriptures humans, too, are depicted as busy at work - whether it be the first characters of the Book of *Genesis*, or Jesus, Martha or Paul in the New Testament.

Work is obviously a human activity, but it can transcend into a divine activity when directed to the glory of God and the good of all humankind.

In the beginning

The Book of *Genesis* is figurative but inspired. The order of events is significant; *Genesis* proclaims human beings as the stewards and, indeed, the crown and summit of God's creation, but makes clear the source of essential means necessary to support human society, in the form of arts and crafts, before they are introduced into the sacred writings. This source is God the mighty creator, and the shaper and worker of all things. Humankind is invited to become co-creator with the one from whom all things are made.

It is by God and from God that our creation has its origin and wonder. In the last act of creation (*Genesis* 1:27-2:4), God created the human race:

> 'So God created humankind in his image, in the image of God he created them; male and female he created them. God blessed them, saying to them, "Be fruitful and multiply, and fill the earth and subdue it; and have dominion over the fish of the sea and over the birds of the air and over every living thing that moves on the earth." God said, "See, I have given you every plant yielding seed that is upon the face of all the earth, and every tree with seed in its fruit; you shall have them for food. And to every beast of the earth, and to every bird of the air, and to everything that has the breath of life, I have given every green plant for food." And so it was. God saw everything that he had made, and indeed, it was very good. And there was evening and there was morning, the sixth day.

> 'Thus the heavens and the earth were finished, and all their multitude. And on the seventh day God finished the work that he had done, and he rested on the seventh day from all the work he had done. So God blessed the seventh day and hallowed it, because on it God had rested from all the work he had done in creation.'

Though the Bible in general does not develop a systematic treatment of work as part of the divine plan for humankind, it presents a broad picture that clearly demonstrates how work is a constitutive part of God's purpose for our race. Indeed, the primitive narrative of the origins of God's will for humanity make quite explicit the task the Creator placed on the earliest men and women in shaping his creation:

> 'The Lord God planted a garden in Eden, in the east; and there he put the man whom he had formed. Out of the ground the Lord God made to grow every tree that is pleasant to the sight and good for food, the tree of life also in the midst of the garden, and the tree of the knowledge of good and evil. ... The Lord God took the man and put him in the garden of Eden to till it and keep it. And the Lord God commanded the man, "You may freely eat of every tree of the garden; but of the tree of the knowledge of good and evil you shall not eat, for in the day that you eat of it you shall die."'
>
> (Genesis 2:8-9,15-17)

After the Fall

According to the *Catechism of the Catholic Church*, the Fall was 'a primeval event, a deed that took place at the beginning of history'. A consequence of this original fault was a break in the harmony between humans and creation. After the Fall, the work of shaping the earth came with a burden attached to it that culminated in death. But not even a tragedy so grave as the Fall was to end the dominion over creation that God had given to humanity.

> 'To the man he said, "Because you have listened to the voice of your wife, and have eaten of the tree about which I commanded you not to, cursed is the ground because of you; in toil you shall eat of it all the days of your life; thorns and thistles it shall bring forth for you; and you shall eat the plants of the field. By the sweat of your face you shall eat bread until you return to the ground, for out of it you were taken; you are dust, and to dust you shall return."'
>
> (Genesis 3:17-19)

It is clear from the writings of the Old Testament and the rabbinic literature that work, in spite of its onerous dimension, was regarded as an opportunity for humankind to fulfil the divine will of God. This remains the case today.

A new covenant

The conviction that the work of humans can also be the work of God is expressed by St Paul, a Jew brought up in the austerity of the rabbinic school of his day, and who later became arguably the most important missionary in history. Paul discusses work in a letter to converts in Thessalonica, Greece, after first speaking about the need to live chaste lives and to love the church community. 'We urge you to aspire to live quietly, to mind your own affairs, and to work with your hands,' he insists (*1 Thessalonians* 4:10-11).

In his second letter to the Thessalonians, St Paul stresses further the importance and centrality of work in the divine plan.

> 'We command you, in the name of our Lord Jesus Christ, to keep away from believers who are living in idleness and not according to the tradition that they have received from us. For you yourselves know how you ought to imitate us; we were not idle when we were with you, and we did not eat anyone's bread without paying for it; but with toil and labour we worked night and day, so that we might not burden any of you. This was not because we do not have that right, but in order to give you an example to imitate. Even when we were with you, we gave you this command: anyone unwilling to work should not eat. For we hear that some of you are living in idleness, mere busybodies, not doing any work. Now such persons we command and exhort in the Lord Jesus Christ to do their work quietly and to earn their own living.'
>
> (*2 Thessalonians* 3:6-12)

St Paul may give the impression of preaching a rather grim 'work ethic', but the apostle, instead of recommending a type of Christian 'respectability' or advocating some kind of political policy, is pointing towards a whole manner of life which both demonstrates and supports the life of faith to which every baptised person is called.

Paul goes a step further in his letter to the Christians at Ephesus by suggesting that manual work, or labour, is a suitable remedy for individualist, self-indulgent and dishonest styles of life:

'Now this I affirm and insist on in the Lord; you must no longer live as the Gentiles live, in the futility of their minds. They are darkened in their understanding, alienated from the life of God because of their ignorance and hardness of heart. They have lost all sensitivity and have abandoned themselves to licentiousness, greedy to practise every kind of impurity. That is not the way you learned Christ! For surely you have heard about him and were taught in him, as truth is in Jesus. You were taught to put away your former way of life, you old self, corrupt and deluded by its lusts, and to be renewed in the spirit of your minds, and to clothe yourselves with the new self, created according to the likeness of God in true righteousness and holiness.

'So then, putting away falsehood, let all of us speak the truth to our neighbours, for we are members of one another. Be angry but do not sin; do not let the sun go down on your anger, and do not make room for the devil. Thieves must give up stealing; rather let them labour and work honestly with their own hands, so as to have something to share with the needy. Let no evil talk come out of your mouths, but only what is useful for building up, as there is need, so that your words may give grace to those who hear. And do not grieve the Holy Spirit of God, with which you were marked with a seal for the day of redemption. Put away from you all bitterness and wrath and anger and wrangling and slander, together with all malice, and be kind to one another, tender-hearted, forgiving one another, as God in Christ has forgiven you.'

(Ephesians 4:17-32)

Take Jesus, for example

The Church has developed a Gospel of Work though references to work in the New Testament are few and far between. Nevertheless, the most significant of all the testimonies to the divine purpose of work can still be found in the accounts of the life of Jesus himself. Throughout most of his adult life, Jesus was a worker in Nazareth.

> 'When Jesus had finished these parables, he left that place. He came to his home town and began to teach the people in their synagogue, so that they were astounded and said, "Where did this man get this wisdom and these deeds of power? Is not this the carpenter's son? Is not his mother called Mary? And are not his brothers James and Joseph and Simon and Judas? And are not all his sisters with us? Where then did this man get all this?" And they took offence at him. But Jesus said to them, "Prophets are not without honour except in their own country and in their own house." And he did not work many miracles there, because of their unbelief.'

(Matthew 13:53-58)

In the parallel text in St Mark's Gospel (6:1-4), Jesus is simply described as the 'carpenter' or 'craftsman' of Nazareth.

Toward the 'new revolution'

The Church has developed its teaching from the teaching of Christ. It is abundantly clear from the parables that Jesus was a close observer of the simple people who made their living by their own labour or by the service of those who were either richer or more powerful. Indeed, it was from the likes of peasants and fishermen that Jesus chose his apostles. Jesus was not a political figure. He did not extol manual work, nor did he condemn trading or profit as such. But he did reject - often in very absolute terms - the oppression or denial of the dignity of human beings in connection with work or trade. In addition, he preached a spiritual poverty ('blessed are the poor of spirit') based first and foremost on the love of God before all else, warning of the danger of worldly attachments and of allowing our hearts to be captured and enslaved by such things as money and possessions. He did not deny, however, that these things had their uses, but rather suggested a right order of things.

Moreover, the social organisation of the society into which Jesus and his followers were born twenty centuries ago was very different from those that we experience in the lands of the free democracies. Again, there is no indication in the scriptures that Jesus intended to change the social system or political order of his times. St Paul, in his epistles, was focused on something quite different: namely God's relationship with men and women; the supernatural and creative aspects of human work, and the rights and responsibilities which accompany it. These questions remain as pertinent today as they did then.

The Gospel of Work flows as a direct consequence of the life and teaching of Jesus Christ. The slow process of the evolution of formal teaching or statements on work and the workers is a strong indication that the Church, in response to the circumstances of the age, meditated upon the implications of the teaching of Christ on human dignity and the divine purpose of God for creation. As the world of work has developed and progressed through its various historical stages, so too has the teaching of the Church on God's purpose for humankind in shaping his creation through work finally come to maturity.

2. The Church's teaching on work

'Work is more than a way of making a living: it is a vocation, a participation in God's creative activity. Work increases the common good. The creation of wealth by productive action is blessed by God and praised by the Church, as both a right and a duty.'

(The Common Good, n. 90)

What is revelation?

Revelation is the central source of Church teaching. We can know through God's works and through the natural light of reason that God exists. We also know that God exists because he told us so himself. The Second Vatican Council document on divine revelation, *Dei Verbum*, reminds the Church that God has shown himself to humankind in many ways. At the heart of this self-revelation by God is the person and teaching of Jesus Christ. Jesus is central to the loving act of God showing himself. This is revelation. There will be no further public revelation by God until Jesus returns at the end of time.

God has shown himself to the Church so that it in turn can respond to the great gift of revelation. Primarily, this means that the Church must explore and reflect on the truths conveyed by God about himself and his purpose for the human race.

Revelation motivates humankind to two specific responses. The first manifests itself in the desire for reflection, meditation and prayer about Jesus Christ and his teaching. In this way, and by exploring the mystery of Jesus in his actions and words, the divine purpose and the wonder of the divine nature become clearer.

The second response is to be found in the experience of the human race as it develops through the ages in creation. As the human race progresses - not only in its material control of creation, but also in its own organisation and self-understanding - many new questions demand answers from the Church. In providing them, the Church fulfils its duty of preserving the truth about God and teaching what God wants for the human race.

> 'Thus the apostolic preaching, which is expressed in a special manner in the inspired books, had to be preserved by a continuous succession until the end of time. Hence the apostles, in handing on what they had themselves received, instruct the faithful to hold fast to the traditions they have learned, either by word of mouth or by letter (cf. *2 Thessalonians* 2:15) and to contend earnestly for the faith once and for all delivered to them (cf. *Jude* 3). That which the apostles transmitted includes everything that contributes towards holiness of life in the People of God, and to the increase of their faith. And so the Church in its doctrine, life and worship perpetuates and hands on to all generations to come, all that it is and believes.

> 'This tradition which comes from the apostles, progresses with the assistance of the Holy Spirit in the Church, in so far as the understanding both of the events and of the words transmitted grows, both by reflection and study on the part of the faithful who ponder them in their hearts (cf. *Luke* 2:19,51), and from a more profound experienced penetration of spiritual matters, as also through the preaching of those who have received with the episcopal succession an assured spiritual gift of truth. The Church, in the course of centuries, tends perpetually towards the fullness of divine truth, until the words of God shall find their complete expression in it.'

> (*Dei Verbum*, n. 8)

The two motives for the exploration of Revelation go hand in hand, but sometimes develop at different paces and in different ways. This exploration sometimes has to wait for an event or experience in the

Church, human race or history for it to take place. This is often the case with work, and the purpose for humanity that is achieved and fulfilled through work.

Guided by the Holy Spirit

The Gospel of Work - the teaching of the Church on work and God's purpose for work - derives from reflection upon Jesus' own life and teachings, and the meditation of the Church on this reality, compounded by the response of the Church, in the lives of its members, to the ever-changing human experience of work. As the human race has developed in its use and control of creation, the teaching of the Church has developed and grown - under the guidance of the Holy Spirit - in understanding the place and meaning of work in God's plan for the human race.

The teaching of the Church on work has developed radically in the last two hundred years, a period marked by huge and dramatic upheavals, or 'revolutions', in the world of work. One of the earliest of these was known as 'the industrial revolution', and the latest has been dubbed the 'information technology revolution'. They have opened up horizons in humanity's approach to work, both individually and collectively, that could scarcely have been previously envisaged.

The bishops, who as the successors to the apostles have a special duty to Christ to preserve and present revelation, to guide on matters of faith and morals, have played their part in developing the response of the Church's teaching.

In the nineteenth century, the bishops tended to focus upon those experiences of work which appeared to be contrary to human dignity. In a series of encyclical letters, the popes identified and condemned injustices that accompanied the industrialisation and urbanisation of society. These teachings culminated in the great encyclical of 1891, *Rerum*

Novarum ('new beginnings'), in which Pope Leo XIII urged people to strive to eliminate oppressive injustice in the workplace, which was then blighting many of the enterprises across the industrialised world. The teaching of the Church continues to remind every person involved in the working world to be ever vigilant to those circumstances which are an affront to human dignity and which therefore must be eradicated.

'The first task is to save the wretched workers from the brutality of those who make use of human beings as mere instruments for the unrestrained acquisition of wealth. It is evident that neither justice nor common humanity permits some men to impose upon others such a heavy burden of labour as will stupefy their minds and exhaust their bodies. A man's ability to work is limited, as is his nature, and there is a point beyond which he cannot go. He can develop his strength by training and use, but only if he obeys the rule of limited spells and frequent periods of rest. Care must be taken, therefore, not to lengthen the working day beyond a man's capacity. How much time there must be for rest depends upon the type of work, the circumstances of the time and place and, particularly, the health of the workers. There must be appropriately shorter hours of work in occupations, such as mining for coal and quarrying iron and the like, where the burden of labour is particularly heavy and also injurious to health. Account should be taken also of the seasons of the year, for often what can be done easily at one time becomes quite impossible or extremely difficult at another. ...

'The general rule is that the greater the burden of labour the greater must be the provision for rest and recuperation: what work has taken away, rest from work must restore. In any contract made between employers and employed there is always the explicit or implicit condition that opportunities must be provided for both rest and recuperation. Any other agreement would be unjust.'

(*Rerum Novarum*, n. 33)

Joy and hope

In the twentieth century, particularly in the post-war era, the Church shifted its focus away from injustice in the world of work, turning its attention instead to questions about the nature of work itself and its role in God's plan. The Second Vatican Council both proclaimed and developed the Church's understanding of the purpose for which God had constituted the human being as his associate in the work of shaping creation.

This was contained in one of the council's greatest documents, the pastoral constitution on the Church in the modern world, often better known simply as *Gaudium et Spes*, which means 'joy and hope'. In this constitution, the fathers of the Council laid the foundation for a vision of the human being as a continuation of the work of God's creation. They discerned in work the processes and means by which God's creation could more completely praise his infinite goodness and give him glory.

'Believers are clear that human enterprise, individual and collective, the enormous effort by which men and women in the course of centuries have improved their living conditions, in itself answers to God's design. Humankind, created in God's image, was commanded to subdue the earth and everything in it, to rule the world in justice and holiness, to refer all things to God as the acknowledged Creator so that the name of God should be honoured over the whole earth.

'This has a profound bearing on everyday tasks. Men and women who provide sustenance for themselves and their families in such a way that at the same time they employ their energies for the benefit of society are justified in thinking that by their own labour they advance the work of the Creator and benefit their fellows, and that their personal industry contributes to the carrying out of the divine plan in history.

'Christians then, far from supposing that the achievements of human skill and power are opposed to the power of God, as though the rational creature were a rival of the Creator, are convinced rather that humankind's triumphs are signs of God's greatness and the fruit of his sublime plan. But the greater the power of men and women the wider their responsibility, whether as single persons or in community. So the Christian message does not distract them from building up the world nor induce them to neglect the welfare of their fellows, but rather obliges them more strictly to these tasks.'

(*Gaudium et Spes*, n. 34)

Work, the family and society

The initiative started in *Gaudium et Spes* has been continued in the teaching of modern popes: John XXIII, Paul VI and John Paul II. In the 1981 encyclical letter on human work, *Laborem Exercens*, Pope John Paul went to special lengths to develop and increase the Church's understanding of how work can provide for the growth of every human being and how it ideally underpins the healthy flourishing of society in the perfect fulfilment of God's purpose:

'Having thus confirmed the personal dimension of human work, we must go on to the second sphere of values which is necessarily linked to work. Work constitutes a foundation for the formation of family life, which is a natural right and something that man is called to. These two spheres of values - one linked to work and the other consequent on the family nature of human life - must be properly united and must permeate each other. In a way, work is a condition for making it possible to found a family, since the family requires the means of subsistence which man normally gains through work. Work and industriousness also influence the whole process of education in the family, for the very reason that everyone "becomes a human being" through, among other things, work, and becoming a human being is precisely the main purpose of the whole process of education. Obviously, two aspects of work in a sense come into play here: the one making family life and its upkeep possible, and the other making possible the achievement of the purposes of the family, especially education. Nevertheless, these two aspects of work are linked to one another and are mutually complementary in various points.

'It must be remembered and affirmed that the family constitutes one of the most important terms of reference for shaping the social and ethical order of human work. The teaching of the Church has always devoted special attention to this question, and in the present document we shall have to return to it. In fact, the family is simultaneously a community made possible by work and the first school of work, within the home, for every person.

'The third sphere of values that emerges from this point of view - that of the subject of work - concerns the great society to which man belongs on the basis of particular cultural and historical links. This society - even when it has not yet taken on the mature form of a nation - is not only the great "educator" of every man, even though an indirect one (because each individual absorbs with the family the contents and values that go to make up the culture of a given nation); it is also a great historical and social incarnation of the work of all generations. All of this brings it about that man combines his deepest human identity with membership of a nation, and intends his work also to increase the common good developed together with his compatriots, thus realising that in this way work serves to add to the heritage of the whole human family, of all the people living in the world.

'These three spheres are always important for human work in its subjective dimension. And this dimension, that is to say, the concrete reality of the worker, takes precedence over the objective dimension. In the subjective dimension there is realised, first of all, that "dominion" over the world of nature to which man is called from the beginning according to the words of the Book of *Genesis*. The very process of "subduing the earth", that is to say work, is marked in the course of history, and especially in recent centuries, by an immense development of technological means. This is an advantageous and positive phenomenon, on condition that the objective dimension of work does not gain the upper hand over the subjective dimension, depriving man of his dignity and inalienable rights or reducing them.'

(*Laborem Exercens*, n. 10)

Final purposes of work

The insights of the Church into God's purpose in giving the human race the capacity and duty of work serve a vital role. In short, they form part of the information and the set of convictions needed by the human family for its very welfare, as well as making an enormous contribution to the many challenges presented in the world of work.

Work in one sense is never neutral. It does more than simply provide the opportunity of maintaining a person in life, or of helping others to provide for themselves. It has great consequences for social organisation. Questions of rights and wrongs, of duties and opportunities, are thus constantly raised. They are often very challenging and strike at the very heart of society.

Some people will assume that these questions can be better addressed without reference to God or his purpose for the human race. The Church argues that such opinions will inevitably lead to poor judgements and, in some cases, disaster in human social organisation - from which will flow injustices and oppression for many people.

But whether a person is an active worker or not, all human beings have both the opportunity and the duty to reflect and act on issues of work, and to keep in mind their consequences for individuals and societies. This is especially the case for people who have the benefit of being baptised and guided by the Holy Spirit in the Church, and who believe that God created men and women ultimately so that they could know, love and serve him.

Because work is a human activity, so closely a part of this world, it is crucial to never lose sight of how work itself also relates to God and how it must be directed towards him because it is part of his plan.

'Re-reading this teaching on the right to property and the common destination of material wealth as it applies to the present times, the question can be raised concerning the origin of the material goods which sustain human life, satisfy people's needs and are an object of their rights.

'The original source of all that is good is the very act of God, who created both the earth and man, and who gave the earth to man so that he might have dominion over it by his work and enjoy its fruits (*Genesis* 1:28). God gave the earth to the whole human race for the sustenance of all its members, without excluding or favouring anyone. This is the foundation of the universal destination of the earth's goods. The earth, by reason of its fruitfulness and its capacity to satisfy human needs, is God's first gift for the sustenance of human life.

'But the earth does not yield its fruits without a particular human response to God's gift, that is to say, without work. It is through work that man, using his intelligence and exercising his freedom, succeeds in dominating the earth and making it a fitting home. In this way, he makes part of the earth his own, precisely the part which he has acquired through work; this is the origin of individual property. Obviously, he also has the responsibility not to hinder others from having their own part of God's gift; indeed, he must co-operate with others so that together all can dominate the earth.

'In history, these two factors - work and the land - are to be found at the beginning of every human society. However, they do not always stand in the same relationship to each other. At one time the natural fruitfulness of the earth appeared to be, and was in fact, the primary factor of wealth, while work was, as it were, the help and support of this fruitfulness. In our time, the role of human work is becoming increasingly important as the productive factor both of non-material and of material wealth. Moreover, it is becoming clearer how a person's work is naturally inter-related with the work of others. More than ever, work is work with others and work for others: it is a matter of doing something for someone else. Work becomes ever more fruitful and productive to the extent that people become more knowledgeable of the productive potentialities of the earth and more profoundly cognisant of the needs of those for whom their work is done.

'In our time, in particular, there exists another form of ownership which is becoming no less important than land: the possession of know-how, technology and skill. The wealth of the industrialised nations is based much more on this kind of ownership than on natural resources.'

(*Centesimus Annus*, nn. 31-32)

A spirituality of work

Work always harbours one danger in particular. It is a prime way of creating wealth, and so presents the risk of serving only to fill the human horizon with a lust for wealth and possessions which grasps hold of the human heart, choking out the higher and more fulfilling call to know, love and serve God the creator, which we do in serving each other.

A spirituality of work is therefore vital for human beings. It is a gift and necessity firstly for those people who already have the inestimable gift of being Christians and members of the Church because it will constantly remind them of the place that work occupies in God's plan for the human race.

However, reflection on the Church's teaching as it continually develops and presents the Gospel of Work through revelation, and the experience of the Church over many centuries, is nevertheless a key for each human being to unlock a door leading to the riches of God's purpose for the whole of the human race.

It is an immeasurable gift and blessing for individuals to understand how humankind must shape creation according to the divine will and to participate in that divine project. Furthermore, tragedies associated with the world of work can be cured and future dangers avoided if human beings individually and collectively understand their purpose and privilege as co-operative instruments of God's creative power; that they are invited to join with God in a kind of co-creative role that is limited but nonetheless real, and that they are called to shape creation to its ultimate purpose which is to give praise and glory to God.

3. Human dignity and the value of work

'We're all sacred in the image of God - those who sweep the floor and carry the stretchers in the hospital, ambulance drivers, the nurses who make the patients comfortable, the home health aids who are so very badly paid. Each is a human person.'
(Cardinal John O'Connor of New York)

Sanctification of work

Work is an essential part of our humanity. We are called to work as part of our human identity. Work has a significance and value in our lives through its acts of creativity, sense of community and opportunity to provide for ourselves, our families and society. The call to work is universal and as part of God's plan, it not only transforms creation, but helps people to fully realise their dignity and to increase it. Through the application of the teachings of Jesus Christ in the workplace and the offering of human labour to the glory of God and the good of all people, our work can be sanctified and made holy.

Work can sanctify people by providing a means to serve God and to serve others, and in so doing to cultivate the virtues, to increase their dignity, and to strive for social justice and the common good. This is achieved by preparing ourselves through prayer, by reading the scriptures, and by receiving the sacraments. It is achieved ultimately through applying, serving and bearing witness to the Gospel of Jesus Christ.

Self-sacrifice and the service of others

'By the sweat of your face you shall eat bread'. These words come from the Book of *Genesis* (3:19) and refer to the toil that has become a characteristic of human work since the Fall. Like prayer, work demands effort. In work, this effort is both an effort of the will and often of the physical self and the mind. It is through such efforts that we are able to direct our thoughts and activities toward God. Pope John Paul II's encyclical, *Laborem Exercens*, reminds us that 'in spite of this toil', which is experienced by all people, 'work is a good thing for man'.

If we are to love God and neighbour through work, it is important, as far as practically possible, to put ourselves and our labours at the service of others. This might, for example, be through creating wealth which benefits the whole community; or it might be through passing on our experience and knowledge in training other people as professionals. It might be simply in serving our employers to the best of our ability, or in providing for those who are dependent on us.

Constant self-sacrifice and the conscientious service of others provides workers with the opportunity to develop personally in the virtues; in particular, humility, the virtue under which all the others flow and flourish.

Work, therefore, offers people the potential to become more fully human, to grow in maturity and in empathetic relationships with each other; to value more the creation which they are privileged to have a role in shaping for the good of each other and to the glory of God.

The model of self-sacrifice and the service of others is Jesus Christ himself. Our Lord stressed the value of service in his teachings, telling his followers that 'the greatest among you must become like the youngest, and the leader like the one who serves' (*Luke* 22:24). He set an example by washing the feet of Peter, and exhorted his disciples to deny themselves, to 'take up their cross' and to follow him (*Matthew* 16:24).

The expression of the self-sacrificial love of Jesus - of God himself - is eloquently captured by St Paul in his letter to the Philippians:

'Do nothing from selfish ambition or conceit, but in humility regard others as better than yourselves. Let each of you look not to your own interests, but to the interests of others. Let the same mind be in you that was in Christ Jesus, who though he was in the form of God, did not regard equality with God as something to be exploited, but emptied himself, taking the form of a slave, being born in human likeness. And being found in human form, he humbled himself and became obedient to the point of death - even death on a cross.'

(*Philippians* 2:3-9)

Activities which are self-sacrifice and directed to the service of God and humankind, through work or otherwise, are essentially creative because by their very nature they have the potential to become transcendental. They look beyond and seek something higher than self-gratification.

An expression of human dignity

It was Dag Hammarskjold, the second Secretary General of the United Nations, who said: 'In our era, the road to holiness necessarily passes through the world of action.'

The Church, in its tradition of social teaching, recognises the value of work and its potential to sanctify, or make holy. It does this by firstly expressing human dignity and then increasing it by the cultivation of the virtues, or moral habits, among which the Church includes the 'virtue of industriousness'.

'Work is a good thing for man. It is not only good in the sense that it is useful or something to enjoy; it is also good as being something worthy, that is to say, something that corresponds to man's dignity, that expresses this dignity and increases it. If one wishes to define more clearly the ethical meaning of work, it is this truth that one must particularly keep in mind. Work is a good thing for man - a good thing for his humanity - because through work man not only transforms nature, adapting it to his own needs, but he also achieves fulfilment as a human being and indeed, in a sense, becomes "more a human being".'

(Laborem Exercens, n. 9)

Besides providing for basic needs, work should also provide people with the opportunity to develop individual talents, and more importantly to claim the fundamental rights and responsibilities that correspond with innate human dignity. Such rights, for example, include the right to a family and the right to private property.

'Men and women have the natural right to share in the benefits of culture, and hence to receive a good general education, and a technical or professional training consistent with the degree of educational development in their own country. Furthermore, a system must be devised for affording gifted members of society the opportunity of engaging in more advanced studies, with a view to their occupying, as far as possible, positions of responsibility in society adequate to their intelligence and acquired skill.'

(Pacem in Terris, n. 13)

Work, therefore, gives a person the means to become an active member and stakeholder of the society in which he or she lives. In turn, they help to shape it through their direct activity - and indirectly through the taxes payable to the state. Indeed, it is because 'work is a good thing for man' that unemployment is such a devastating and tragic evil.

'Man must work, both because the Creator has commanded it and because of his own humanity, which requires work in order to be maintained and developed. Man must work out of regard for others, especially his own family, but also for the society he belongs to, the country of which he is a child, and the whole human family of which he is a member, since he is the heir to the work of generations and at the same time a sharer in building the future of those who will come after him in the succession of history. All this constitutes the moral obligation of work, understood in its wide sense. When we have to consider the moral rights, corresponding to this obligation, of every person with regard to work, we must always keep before our eyes the whole vast range of points of reference in which the labour of every working subject is manifested'.

(*Laborem Exercens*, n. 16)

The dignity of workers has traditionally been upheld by the trade unions. George Woodcock, from Bamber Bridge, Lancashire, was one trade union leader who understood the clear bond between human dignity and the world of work, and who dedicated his working life to making the connection ever stronger.

A Catholic, Woodcock was General Secretary of the Trade Union Congress from 1960 to 1969, having joined as secretary of the Research and Economic Department in 1936. He enjoyed a distinguished career as a member of the Royal Commissions and other public bodies before his election as leader. He is recalled as a man who brought to the post dignity, authority and influence which has seldom been equalled since. He raised the public profile of the TUC as an organisation speaking for working people and their families, and sought to reconcile conflicting claims on national and international resources for the common good. Under his leadership, constructive and co-operative relations were developed with Conservative and Labour governments.

These found expression in 1963 in the formation of the National Economic Development Council. Against a background of national consensus concerning economic and social aims, the TUC played a part in the achievement of near full employment and economic growth which was faster and longer sustained than at any time since.

For Woodcock, a central concern was that trade unions should give individual working people a say in the decisions which affected them at work and in society, and which would have a direct impact on their intrinsic dignity. He always insisted on the responsibilities of all trade unions to be accountable to members and not to let extraneous concerns deflect them from their representative role. That did not rule out their taking the responsibility of leadership and planning for the future.

His forthright comments on government policies and actions, which sprung from his industrial experience and penetrating intellect, were feared by Conservative and Labour ministers alike. Though he could be acerbic, he displayed Christian hope and confidence in the underlying goodness of people. His comments on pay restraint at the 1962 TUC Congress, were aimed at both the Conservative government and the Labour opposition which was to take power two years later:

> 'If the government of this country want their citizens to act reasonably, their first object should be to create a mood, an attitude in which people will be readily disposed towards reason, towards responsibility and towards dignity. ... You must get at the roots, get at the things which move people. You must appeal to them, appeal to their sense of responsibility, and then if you do that there may be no limit to what people are prepared to do voluntarily, sensibly in their own interest and in the interests of everybody else.'

Cultivation of the virtues

The *Catechism of the Catholic Church* describes a virtue as 'a habitual and firm disposition to do good'. Christians in particular are called upon to cultivate the virtues in their working lives, chiefly in order to sanctify themselves and their work and to transform their world in accordance with God's holy will.

The moral virtues are grouped around the four cardinal virtues of prudence, justice, fortitude and temperance. Prudence disposes the practical reason to discern, in every circumstance, our true good and to choose the right means for achieving it; justice consists in the firm and constant will to give God and neighbour their due; fortitude ensures firmness in difficulties and constancy in the pursuit of the good; and temperance moderates the attraction of the pleasures of the senses and provides balance in the use of created goods.

Kevin Flanagan, formed by the Young Christian Workers, is clear in his belief too that the cultivation of personal qualities, combined with offering work to God, are the key features of Christian working life. People, he believes, can sanctify their work and themselves by honing such qualities as perseverance, determination, a willingness to work together, endurance, faith, openness and enthusiasm. He said: 'In whatever you are doing as men and women of today, you must turn your office desk, work bench, teacher's desk into your altar where you offer your work to Christ.'

> 'God, who has endowed man with intelligence, imagination and sensitivity, has also given him the means of completing God's work in a certain way: whether he be artist or craftsman, engaged in management, industry or agriculture, everyone who works is a creator. Bent over a material that resists his efforts, a man by his work gives his imprint to it, acquiring as he does so, perseverance, skill and a spirit of invention. Further, when work is done in common, when hope, hardship, ambition and joy are shared, it brings together and firmly unites wills, minds and hearts: in its accomplishments men and women find themselves to be brothers and sisters.'
>
> (Paul VI, *Populorum Progressio*, n. 27)

Work itself is not a guarantor of salvation. But it generally provides the opportunity for each person on a daily basis to make a subjective response to the demand of the Gospel to 'do good and shun evil'. Those who struggle in their working lives to achieve this by serving God and neighbour will grow in the virtues and in holiness, while helping to transform creation in accordance with the divine plan.

Mother Teresa of Calcutta understood that all people were called to holiness - 'even journalists'. St Theresa of Lisieux, one of the greatest of modern saints, espoused a 'little way' to holiness of doing life's most simplest and trivial things with love. Her teaching suggests that all people, no matter what they do for a living, are capable of finding salvation through their working lives.

A call to justice

The Catholic Church sets workers' rights in the broader context of genuine human rights, based on the natural and universal moral law. The Church believes that the world of work challenges people to practice and cultivate in particular the virtues of justice and industriousness, and to link them to the development of fair structures and social orders. The Church makes this demand because work is not always directed to the common good and the glory of God. In other words, work is sometimes used to do evil.

As a result of the Fall, a constant effort is required to ensure that the good of the human person is always the subject of work and the focal point of any economic system, so that even while 'matter may gain in nobility', people 'never experience a lowering of their dignity'.

> 'It is well known that it is possible to use work in various ways against man, that it is possible to punish man with the system of forced labour in concentration camps, that work can be a means for oppressing man, and that in various ways it is possible to exploit human labour, that is to say, the worker. All this pleads in favour of the moral obligation to link industriousness as a virtue with the social order of work, which will enable man to

become, in work, "more a human being" and not be degraded by it not only because of the wearing out of his physical strength (which, up to a certain point is inevitable), but especially through the damage to the dignity and subjectivity that are proper to him.'

(Laborem Exercens, n. 9)

'The Church has the right and the duty to advocate a social order in which the human dignity of all is fostered, and to protest when it is in any way threatened. Thus the Church opposes totalitarianism because it oppresses people and deprives them of their freedom. While recognising the importance of wealth creation, the Church denounces any abuses of economic power such as those which deprive employees of what is needed for a decent standard of living.'

(Cardinal Basil Hume, preface, *The Common Good*)

'Workers have rights which Catholic teaching has consistently maintained are superior to the rights of capital. These include the right to decent work, to just wages, to security of employment, to adequate rest and holidays, to limitation of hours of work, to health and safety protection, to non-discrimination, to form and join trade unions, and, as a last resort, to go on strike. The Catholic Church has always deplored the treatment of employment as nothing more than a form of commercial contract. This leads to a sense of alienation between a worker and his or her labour. Instead, forms of employment should stress the integration of work and worker, and encourage the application of creative skills.'

(*The Common Good*, n. 91)

Pope John Paul II, in *Laborem Exercens*, indicated that the interests of capital and labour were complementary rather than conflicting, and said each should be united in the project of wealth creation, to the enhancement of the good of all people. Nevertheless, the Church has traditionally and consistently supported the role of trade unions in establishing social justice for workers. Today, Catholics are still urged by the Church to join and become active in their appropriate trade union in order to defend their legitimate rights and interests.

Indeed, for more than a hundred years, many Catholics have struggled to put the Church's teaching on the world of work into practice, and many have chosen the trade union movement as a means to achieve this objective. For some the quest for justice has been romantic and even heroic, while for others the price has been far dearer.

The Brazilian, Chico Mendes, was assassinated in 1988 because of his activities on behalf of workers. Mendes was president of the Xapuri Rural Workers, a member of the National Council of Rubber Tappers, and of the National Council of the Trade Union Congress, an activist in the Workers' Party, and a defender of the Amazonian eco-system. He said:

> 'Our movement grew out of the needs of the rubber tappers. We made a lot of mistakes but we learned from them. You know, people have to look after themselves, they have to fight and be creative. … These people are the fruit of our movement's advances. After each stage in the struggle, we evaluate the situation, we learn from our experiences. The struggle teaches us many things. Every day we learn something, while at the same time knowing we could be on the receiving end of a bullet at any time.

> 'We're involved because of our ideals and we'll never turn back. Our roots are too deep for us to think of giving up the struggle. It is a question of honour, a matter of principle. None of us would betray our movement. We all worked together to build up that spirit, that love. They would have to kill us all to destroy our movement and I can't see them managing to do that. I don't get that cold feeling any more. I am no longer afraid of dying and I

know they can't destroy us. If any of us got killed, the resistance would still go on and it might even be that much stronger.'

Cesar Chavez was another Catholic trade union leader who struggled against overwhelming odds to achieve justice for farmworkers. Not only was he successful in achieving his aims, but in August 2000 he was posthumously honoured by the State of California, which has inaugurated a public holiday in his memory. Chavez was a man who became legendary because, although he received a poor education and though he lived a modest life, never owning a home or even a car, he was still able to improve conditions for thousands of low-paid workers.

In the 1960s Chavez began working to create a farm workers' union. Known at first as the National Farm Workers' Association, the union was chartered in 1966 by the American Federation of Labour and the Congress of Industrial Organisations as the United Farm Workers organising committee, with Chavez as its president. In 1968 Chavez gained notoriety as leader of the nationwide boycott of Californian table grapes in a drive to achieve labour contracts. The struggle continued until the 1970s.

Chavez, who died in 1993, directly linked his faith to his quest for justice. Before each march, for example, he would organise a Mass for the farmworkers. A banner of Our Lady of Guadalupe, the patron of the Americas, was at the head of every procession. He once said:

> 'When we are really honest with ourselves, we must admit that our lives are all that really belong to us. So it is how we use our lives that determines what kind of men we are. It is my deepest belief that only by giving our lives do we find life. I am convinced that the truest act of courage, the strongest act of manliness, is to sacrifice ourselves for others in a totally non-violent struggle for justice. To be a man is to struggle for others. God help us to be men.'

Solidarity and subsidiarity

Closely associated with the quest for justice is the principle of solidarity, which allied to the principle of subsidiarity, serves to promote a just social order. The *Catechism* describes solidarity as 'an eminently Christian virtue' which 'practises the sharing of spiritual goods even more than material ones' (nn. 1939-1941):

> 'The principle of solidarity, also articulated in terms of "friendship" or "social charity", is a direct demand of human and Christian brotherhood. Solidarity is manifested in the first place by the distribution of goods and remuneration for work. It also presupposes the effort for a more just social order where tensions are better able to be reduced and conflicts more readily settled by negotiation. Socio-economic problems can be resolved only with the help of all the forms of solidarity: solidarity of the poor among themselves, between rich and poor, of workers among themselves, between employers and employees in a business, solidarity among nations and peoples.'

Pope John Paul II, in his encyclical, *Sollicitudo Rei Socialis*, called solidarity a 'question of interdependence, sensed as a system determining relationships in the contemporary world in its economic, cultural, political and religious elements, and accepted as a moral category' (n. 38):

> 'When interdependence becomes recognised in this way, the correlative response as a moral and social attitude, as a "virtue", is solidarity. This then is not a feeling of vague compassion or shallow distress at the misfortunes of so many people, both near and far. On the contrary it is a firm and persevering determination to commit oneself to the common good; that is to say, to the good of all and of each individual because we are all really responsible for all.'

Lech Walesa can be accredited with helping to establish the understanding of solidarity in the modern mind. An electrician who worked in the Lenin Shipyard in Gdansk, Poland, Walesa became famous around the world because he used the principle of solidarity as an instrument to challenge the totalitarian communist state. Chairman of the Strikes Committees in the 1970s and 1980s, the trade union he went on to found (the National Coordinating Commission of Independent Autonomous Trade Union Solidarity) was even known simply as 'Solidarity'. The collective efforts of Walesa and his followers, both in Poland and overseas, were underpinned by the virtue and principle of solidarity. The fruits of their labours can be seen in the collapse of communism in the 1980s, first in Poland and then throughout the eastern bloc. On winning the Nobel Peace Prize in 1983, in the midst of his struggle, Walesa, a dedicated Catholic, said:

> 'We are fighting for the right of the working people to association and for the dignity of human labour. We respect the dignity and the rights of every man and woman and every nation. The path to a brighter future for the world leads through honest reconciliation of the conflicting interests and not through hatred and bloodshed. To follow that path means to enhance the moral power of the all-embracing idea of human solidarity.'

Solidarity encourages and permits the exercise of power collectively. It is joined with the principle of subsidiarity that demands the dispersal of authority and power to the lowest tiers possible; in order that authorities do not assume for themselves roles which can be competently undertaken by smaller and less powerful bodies.

The common good

The common good is a central concept of Catholic social teaching. It is defined, according to the *Catechism*, as the 'sum total of social conditions which allow people, either as groups or individuals, to reach their fulfilment more fully and more easily'. There are three essential elements to the common good. These are: firstly, the respect for and the promotion of the fundamental rights of the person; then prosperity, or the development of the spiritual and temporal goods of society; and thirdly, the peace and security of the group and of its members.

The *Catechism* teaches that the dignity of the human person requires the pursuit of the common good, which is 'always orientated toward the progress of persons'.

The theme of the common good was embraced by the Catholic bishops of England and Wales in their document, *The Common Good and the Catholic Church's Social Teaching*. The document describes the common good as a 'guarantor of individual rights, and as the necessary public context in which conflicts of individual rights and interests can be adjudicated or reconciled'. Some of these rights pertain to the world of work.

> 'Work increases the common good. The creation of wealth by productive action is blessed by God and praised by the Church, as both a right and a duty. When properly organised and respectful of the humanity of the worker, it is also a source of fulfilment and satisfaction. At best, workers should love the work they do. The treatment of workers must avoid systematically denying them that supreme measure of satisfaction. We would oppose an unduly negative view of work even from a Christian perspective, which would regard it purely as a burden of drudgery; or even worse, a curse consequent upon the Fall. On the contrary, even before the Fall human work was the primary means whereby humanity was to co-operate with and continue the work of the Creator, by responding to God's invitation to "subdue the earth".'
>
> (*The Common Good*, n. 90)

'In our time, the role of human work is becoming increasingly important as the productive factor both of non-material and material wealth. Moreover, it is becoming clearer how a person's work is naturally interrelated with the work of others. More than ever, work is work with others and for others: it is a matter of doing something for someone else. Work becomes ever more fruitful and productive to the extent that people become ever more knowledgeable of the productive potentialities of the earth and more profoundly cognisant of the needs of those for whom their work is done.'

(Centesimus Annus, n. 31)

Dorothy Day (1897-1980) was the founder, along with Peter Maurin, of the Catholic Worker Movement in the USA. From her writings, it is clear that the concept of the common good, as an arbiter of human rights and social justice, was at the heart of her efforts to improve society. The Second Vatican Council document, *Gaudium et Spes*, states that 'the order of things must be subordinate to the order of persons and not the other way around'. The *Catechism* states that this order is founded on truth, built up in justice and animated by love. The following text, written by Day, shows how she understood this reality in her work:

'What we would like to do is change the world - make it a little simpler for people to feed, clothe and shelter themselves as God intended them to do. And, by fighting for better conditions, by crying out unceasingly for the rights of workers, of the poor, of the destitute - the rights of the worthy and the unworthy poor, in other words - we can, to a certain extent, change the world; we can work for the oasis, the little cell of joy and peace in a harried world ... we repeat, there is nothing that we can do but love, and, dear God, please enlarge our hearts to love each other, to love our neighbour, to love our enemy as well as our friend.'

Evangelisation

St Francis of Assisi urged people to go out and preach the Gospel, using words only if they had to. Evangelisation is more than telling people about Jesus and his teachings. It is bearing witness to the Gospel in all that we do; in our daily lives, we can act as living signposts to the glory of the living, loving God and his kingdom.

Since each of us is unique and unrepeatable, endowed with our own set of talents, God calls each of us to serve him in a unique way. Not everyone is called to preach to crowds of thousands, or to give their lives in martyrdom, for example, yet each baptised person is called to bear witness to the Gospel. St Ignatius of Loyola believed that God had a unique purpose for every person; a role only that person could fulfil. But first it was important for the person to rid him or herself of worldly attachments, so that he or she could discern God's purpose for them in his plan for humankind.

> 'In effect, to teach and to spread her social doctrine pertains to the Church's evangelising mission and is an essential part of the Christian message, since this doctrine points out the direct consequences of that message in the life of society and situates daily work and struggles for justice in the context of bearing witness to Christ the Saviour. This doctrine is likewise a source of unity and peace in dealing with the conflicts which inevitably arise in social and economic life. Thus it is possible to meet these new situations without degrading the human person's transcendent dignity, either in oneself or in one's adversaries, and to direct those situations toward just solutions.'
>
> (*Centesimus Annus*, n. 5)

The workplace gives Christians the opportunity to spread the Church's social doctrine through the service of justice and the common good, the cultivation of the virtues, a life of active charity, and a commitment to ordering all material goods and human activities to the glory of God and the common good. The vocation of many people is to be Christian disciples in their working lives.

Salford's Terry Finnigan, who died in 1998 after a long illness, wrote in 1992 on the subject of the decade of evangelisation in the context of his work with the Young Christian Workers and later the Movement of Christian Workers. Summing up his apostleship, Terry said:

> 'Evangelist - the very word sends shivers down my spine; ... if that's what I have to do to be part of the decade of evangelisation, then I'll have to opt out and carry on in my own way serving Christ as best I know how.

> 'As a convenor shop steward, I believe Christ wants me to bring my Christian values to my place of work, in my union duties, in dealing both with management and workers alike. I see no conflict in Christ's teachings and my union activities. Fighting for justice in working conditions, for fair pay, against unjust treatment of workers is part of my service to Christ. Christ would never have shirked his responsibility to the worker who was unjustly treated. Even if he met with opposition from rich high-powered people; he showed us that all through his life on earth. He also showed us that workers too can be greedy, avaricious and lazy. That too I have to take into consideration when dealing with union cases. To help me I do pray for guidance because without God's help I can do nothing. I also meet on a regular basis with a group of Christian trade unionists from my local area and we share our problems in the name of Christ: sharing together is a tremendous help.'

Prayers and meditations

Prayer is an important area of Christian life. The *Catechism of the Catholic Church* adopts the words of St John Damascene in describing prayers as 'the raising of the mind and heart to God or the requesting of good things' (n. 2590). Similarly, the *Catechism* (n. 2743) asserts that it is always possible to pray, citing the words of St John Chrysostom: 'It is possible to offer fervent prayer even while walking in public or strolling alone, or seated in your shop ... while buying or selling ... or even when cooking.'

Of course, it would be foolish to neglect giving proper attention to safety at work. Any attempt at prayer must not be in conflict with the God-given action of work itself. Yet it is remarkable how, even in the minds of Christians, there sometimes exists a false dichotomy between prayer and work, when in fact they complement each other.

Prayer for work and in work starts from the conviction that work is God's good gift to us as human beings commissioned by him to carry out the task of shaping and adorning his creation. Prayer helps us to focus and reflect on this task. We can prepare for work by morning prayer, for example, and meditate, reflect and give thanks for work at the end of the day. To help us to discern and fulfil God's holy will for us and for all people, we can have specific regard in our prayers to the tasks and activities entrusted to us.

The following selection of prayers is intended to enrich and strengthen the bond between prayer and work - both are activities which can each bring people closer to God.

Morning Prayers

Our Father
Our Father, who art in heaven,
Hallowed be thy name.
Thy kingdom come,
Thy will be done on earth as it is in heaven.
Give us this day our daily bread
And forgive our trespasses
as we forgive those who trespass against us.
And lead us not into temptation,
But deliver us from evil.
Amen.

Morning offering
My God, I offer you my thoughts, words, deeds and sufferings this day, and beseech that you give me your grace that I may not offend you but may faithfully serve you and do your holy will in all things.

Intercession
St Joseph the worker, pray for us.

Prayer of St Ignatius of Loyola
Teach us, dear Lord,
To serve you as you deserve to be served;
To give and not to count the cost;
To fight and not to heed the wounds;
To toil and not to count the cost;
And to labour and to seek for no reward
Save for the knowledge that we do your will.
Through Christ Our Lord.
Amen.

Prayer of petition

Dear Lord,
Enlighten my heart and mind with your love
And guide my hand this day
So I may serve you to the best of my ability.
Bless all my activities and undertakings.
Strengthen and protect me,
And give me your grace that I may overcome my weaknesses
And grow in the power to do good
To the glory of your name.
Amen.

From the daily prayer of the Church

Lord God, who entrusted the earth to us to till it and care for it,
and made the sun to serve our needs:
Give us the grace this day to work faithfully for your glory
and for our neighbours' good.
We ask this through Christ Our Lord.
Amen.

General Prayers

To the Father

Father, creator of all that is good,
You have called men and women to work in your world,
And by their co-operation to better the condition of mankind.
Grant that we may always work together as children of your family
And love all people as our brethren.
Through Christ our Lord.
Amen.

For our place of work

Blessed are you, Lord our God,
Creator of the universe and Father of us all.
We praise you for your mighty works.
Look on us with love
And hear our prayers today.
Grant your blessing to this place of work
And to all who work here.
Let their work contribute to the good
of all members of this community.
Father, blessed are you,
For ever and ever.
Amen.

For the use of skill in work

Lord God, you commend the work of humanity in the writings you
gave to your people Israel, saying: 'Men skilled with their hands
without whom no city could be lived in, maintain my ancient
handiwork.'
Grant to us in all the many forms of skills we use that our concern for
the exercise of our skills will be for your glory and to the life of our
fellow human beings.

For peace and harmony at work

God of justice and peace,
Since all resources come from you
Hear the prayer of your Church:
Provide for the needs of both workers and employers
And guide us to solutions fair to all,
That we may work together
In harmony and peace.
Through Christ our Lord.
Amen.

For increased appreciation of work
God our Father,
You have placed all the powers of nature
under the control of humanity and its work.
May we bring the spirit of Christ to all our efforts
And work with our brothers and sisters at our common task,
establishing true love
and guiding your creation to perfect fulfilment.
Through Christ our Lord.
Amen.

For the unemployed
Father of all,
Grant to every person who wants work but cannot find it,
The grace to sustain the suffering of being unemployed,
Together with the hope that in your mercy work will come
So that the dignity of each in shaping this creation
according to your will
Will be preserved
We ask this of you who lives and reigns for ever.
Amen.

Of thanksgiving
Almighty Father,
For the gift of work that you have given us
We thank you.
For the hope that work gives us of the aim
To serve our fellow workers,
And indeed all our fellow human beings,
We offer you thanks.
On those who cannot work or are without work
We ask your mercy to sustain them in their sufferings.
We make our prayer through Christ our Lord.
Amen.

General intercessions

Give courage and strength to the young. Help them to choose their work, and make the right decisions for their way of life.
Lord in your mercy, hear our prayer.

Lord, we give thanks for the order of created things; you have blessed us with the resources of the earth and the gift of human life.
Lord in your mercy, hear our prayer.

We thank you for the beauty of creation; may our work not disfigure it, but enhance it to your greater glory.
Lord in your mercy, hear our prayer.

Lord we give thanks for humanity's share in your continuing work of creation; we praise you for your gifts of inventive skills and creative vision.
Lord in your mercy, hear our prayer.

In the life of your incarnate Son, Lord, you show us the dignity of humanity's labour. With this in mind we ask your blessing on all workers.
Lord in your mercy, hear our prayer.

Bless those who work on the land: may we receive the fruits of the earth with thankfulness.
Lord in your mercy, hear our prayer.

We pray for all those in industry; may they work in harmony for justice and the good of the whole community.
Lord in your mercy, hear our prayer.

Pour out your Spirit, Lord, on artists, craftspeople and musicians; may their abiding work bring variety, joy and inspiration to our lives.
Lord in your mercy, hear our prayer.

We pray for all who are working today; be at their side Lord at home and in the city, in the factory and in the fields.
Lord in your mercy, hear our prayer.

Give us the grace to serve others in our work and find peace when it is time to rest.
Lord in your mercy, hear our prayer.

May Mary, the mother of Jesus and the wife of Joseph, the housewife of the family home at Nazareth, protect us as we say:

Hail Mary, full of grace,
The Lord is with thee.
Blessed art thou among women
And blessed is the fruit of thy womb, Jesus.
Holy Mary, Mother of God,
Pray for us sinners,
Now and at the hour of our death.
Amen.

Heavenly Father,
under the guidance of your Holy Spirit
we have been given the grace to pray
both in praise of your glory
and in request for the abundance of your mercies
upon the human race.
May you grant to each one of us a spirit of loving
co-operation with Jesus the Lord,
the worker of Nazareth, as we seek to prepare for
the day of entry into your eternal kingdom.
We ask this of you who lives and reigns
For ever and ever.
Amen.

Work as an expression of love

Pope John Paul II, apostolic exhortation *Redemptoris Custos* on the person and mission of Saint Joseph in the life of Christ and of the Church, 1989, nn. 22-24.

'Work was the daily expression of love in the life of the family of Nazareth. The Gospel specifies the kind of work Joseph did in order to support his family: he was a carpenter. This simple word sums up Joseph's entire life. For Jesus, these were hidden years, the years to which Luke refers after recounting the episode that occurred in the Temple: "And he went down with them and came to Nazareth, and was obedient to them" (*Luke* 2:51). This "submission" or obedience of Jesus in the house of Nazareth should be understood as a sharing in the work of Joseph. Having learned the work of his presumed father, he was known as "the carpenter's son". If the family of Nazareth is an example and model for human families, in the order of salvation and holiness, so too, by analogy, is Jesus' work at the side of Joseph the carpenter. In our own day, the Church has emphasised this by instituting the liturgical memorial of St Joseph the Worker on May 1. Human work, and especially manual labour, receive special prominence in the Gospel. Along with the humanity of the Son of God, work too has been taken up in the mystery of the incarnation, and has also been redeemed in a special way. At the workbench where he plied his trade together with Jesus, Joseph brought human work closer to the mystery of the redemption.

'In the human growth of Jesus "in wisdom, age and grace," the virtue of industriousness played a notable role, since "work is a human good" which "transforms nature" and makes man "in a sense, more human" (John Paul II, *Laborem Exercens*, n. 9).

'The importance of work in human life demands that its meaning be known and assimilated in order to "help all people to come closer to God, the Creator and Redeemer, to participate in his salvific plan for man and the world, and to deepen … friendship with Christ in their lives, by accepting, through faith, a living participation in his threefold mission as priest, prophet and king" (*Laborem Exercens*, n. 24).

'What is crucially important here is the sanctification of daily life, a sanctification which each person must acquire according to his or her own state, and one which can be promoted according to a model accessible to all people: "St Joseph is the model of those humble ones that Christianity raises up to great destinies; … he is the proof that in order to be a good and genuine follower of Christ, there is no need of great things - it is enough to have the common, simple and human virtues, but they need to be true and authentic" (Paul VI, discourse, 19 March 1969).'

A hymn on work

Take my hands and make them as your own,
And use them for your kingdom here on earth.
Consecrate them to your care,
Anoint them for your service where
You may need your Gospel to be sown.

Take my hands, they speak now for my heart,
And by their actions they will show their love.
Guard them on their daily course,
Be their strength and guiding force
To ever serve the Trinity above.

Take my hands, I give them to you, Lord.
Prepare them for the service of your name.
Open them to human need
And by their love they'll sow your seed
So all may know the love and hope you gave.

Take my hands, take my hands, O Lord.